A,B,C Alphabet Coloring For Kids 4-6

A

APPLE

B

BALL

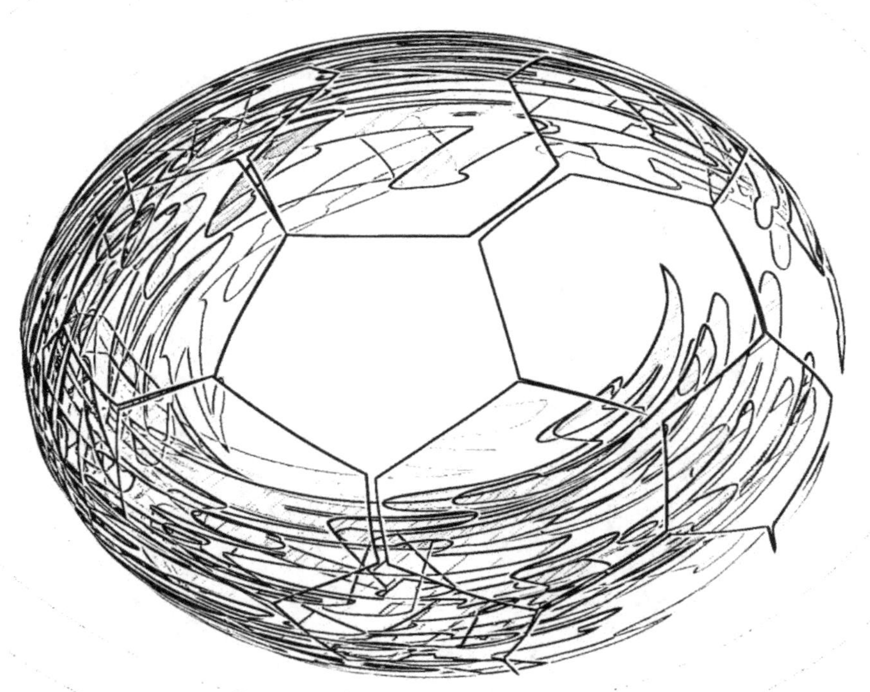

C

CAT

D

DOG

E

EGG

F

FLOWER

G

GORILLA

H

HORSE

I

ICE CREAM

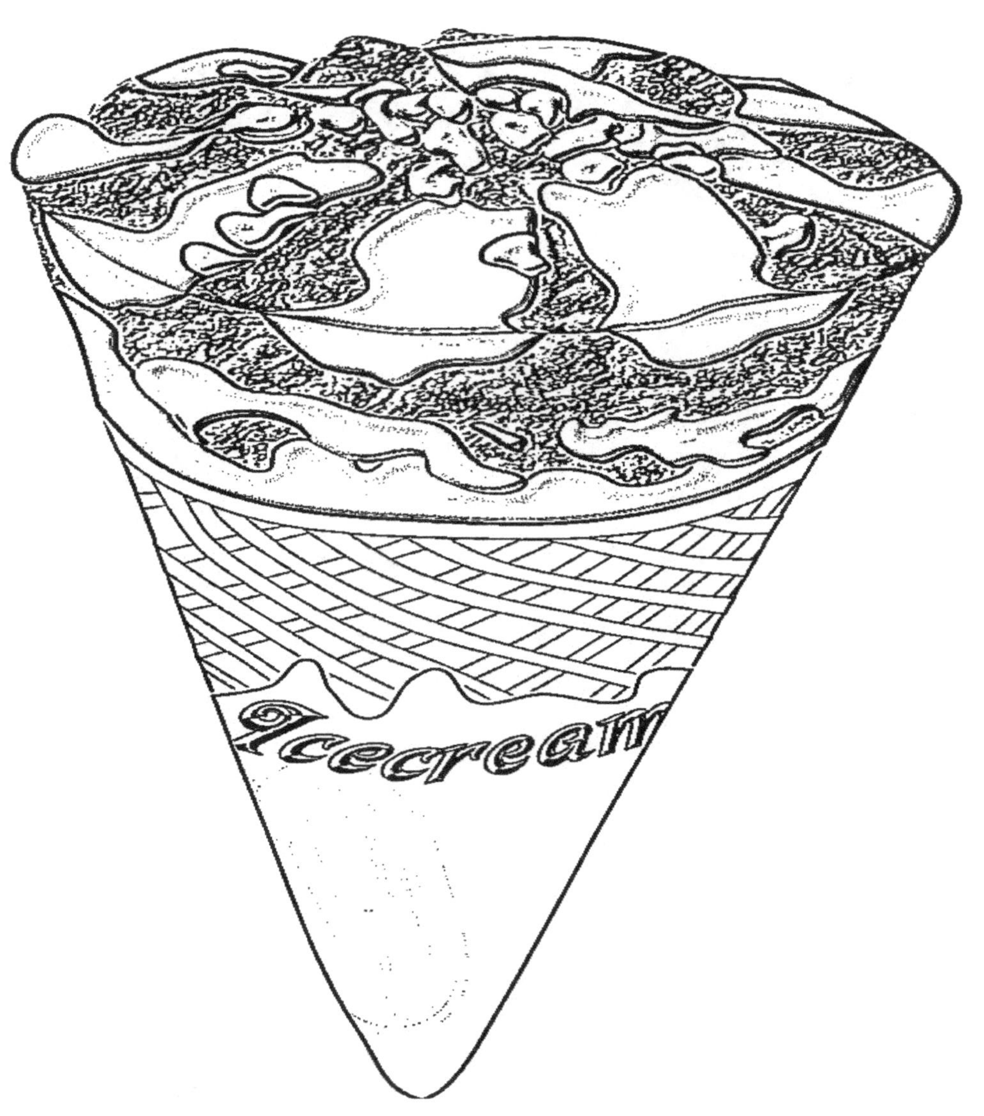

J
JUICE

K

KITE

L

LAMP

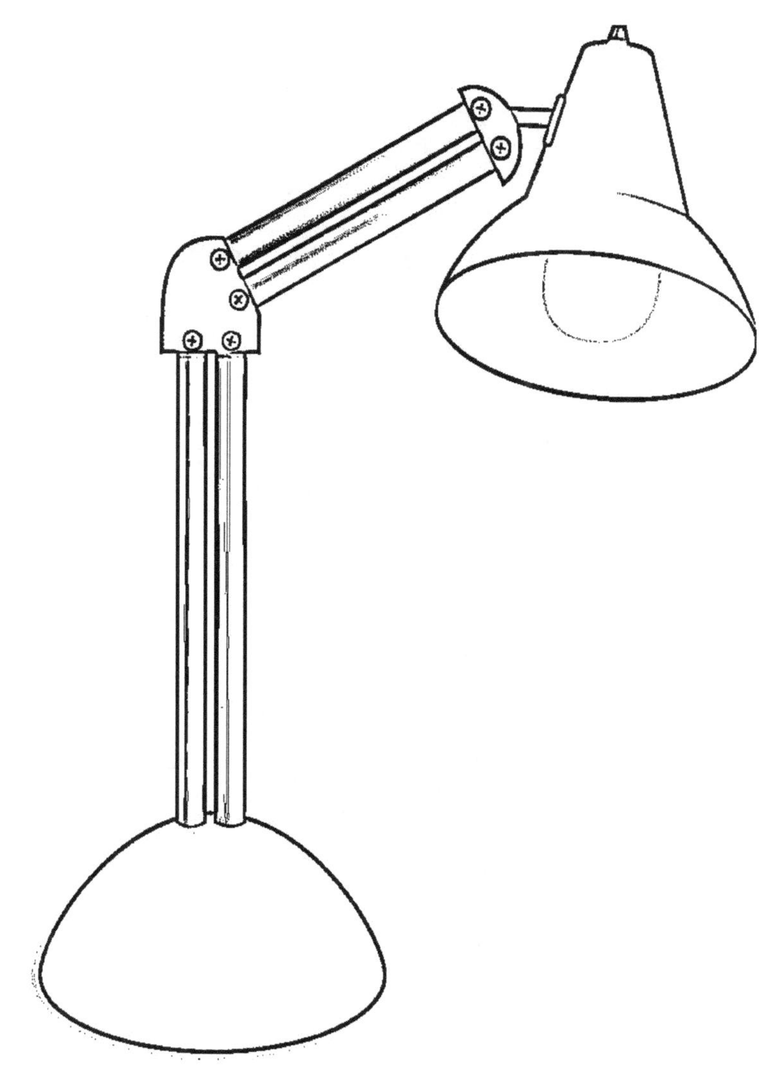

M

MONKEY

N

NET

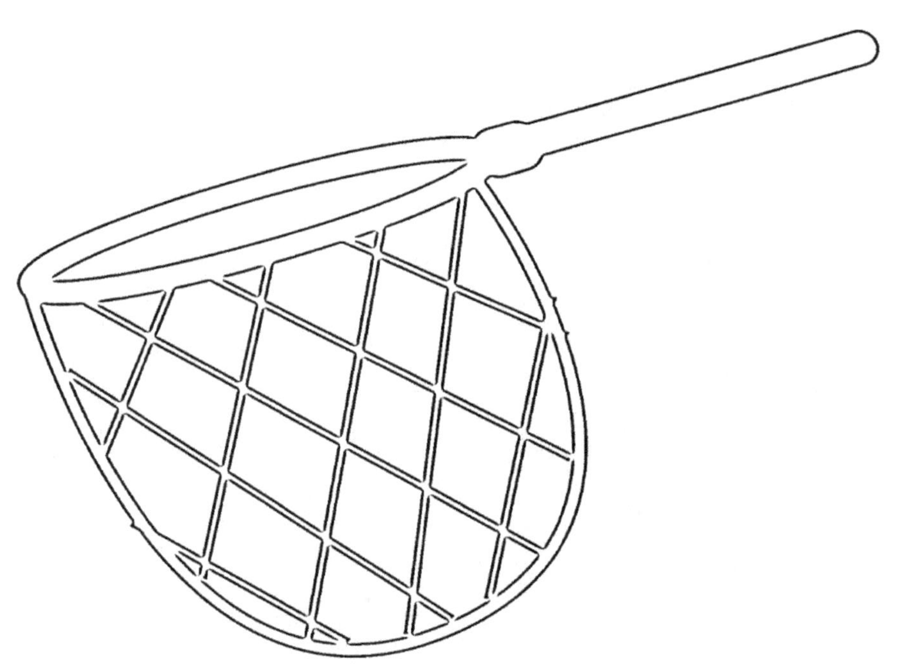

O

ORANGE

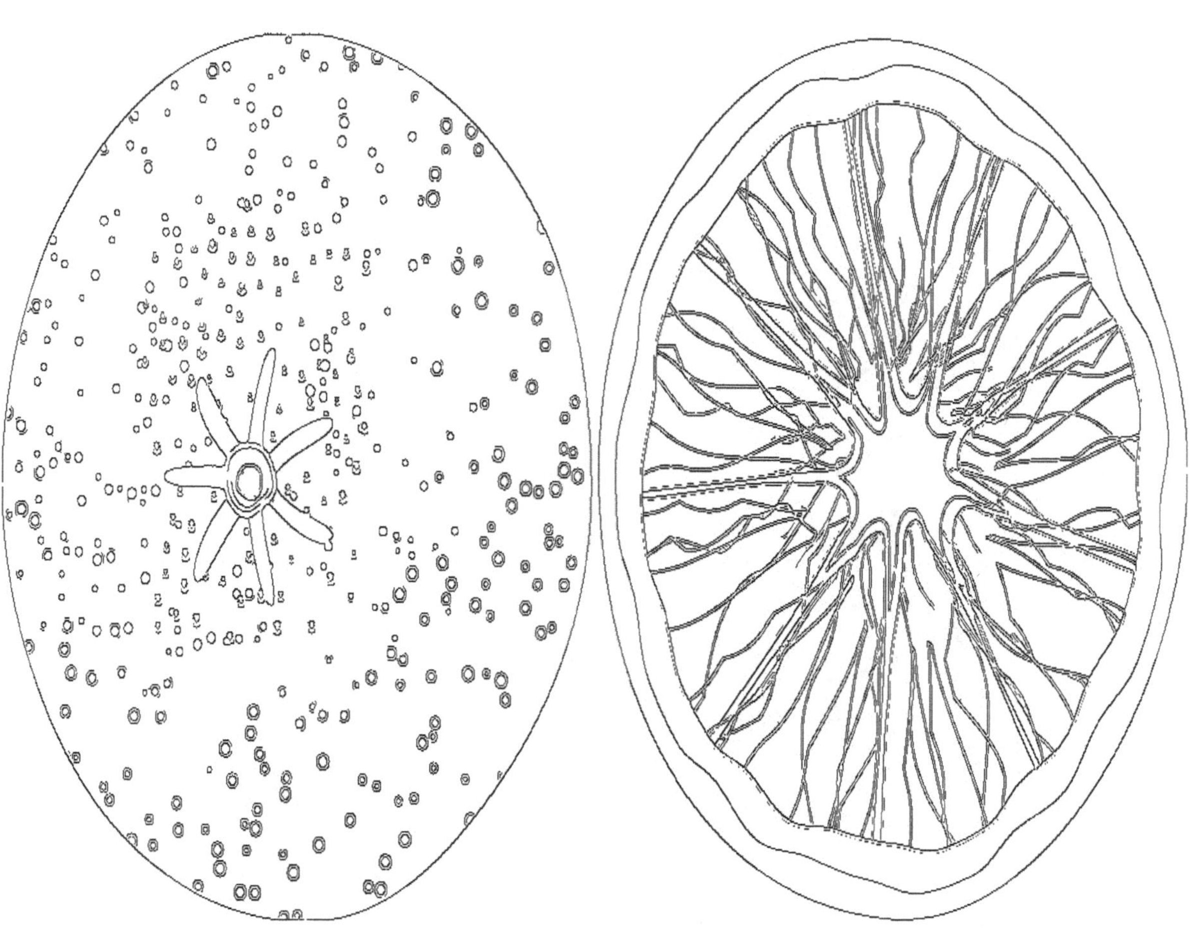

P

PINEAPPLE

Q

QUEEN

R

RING

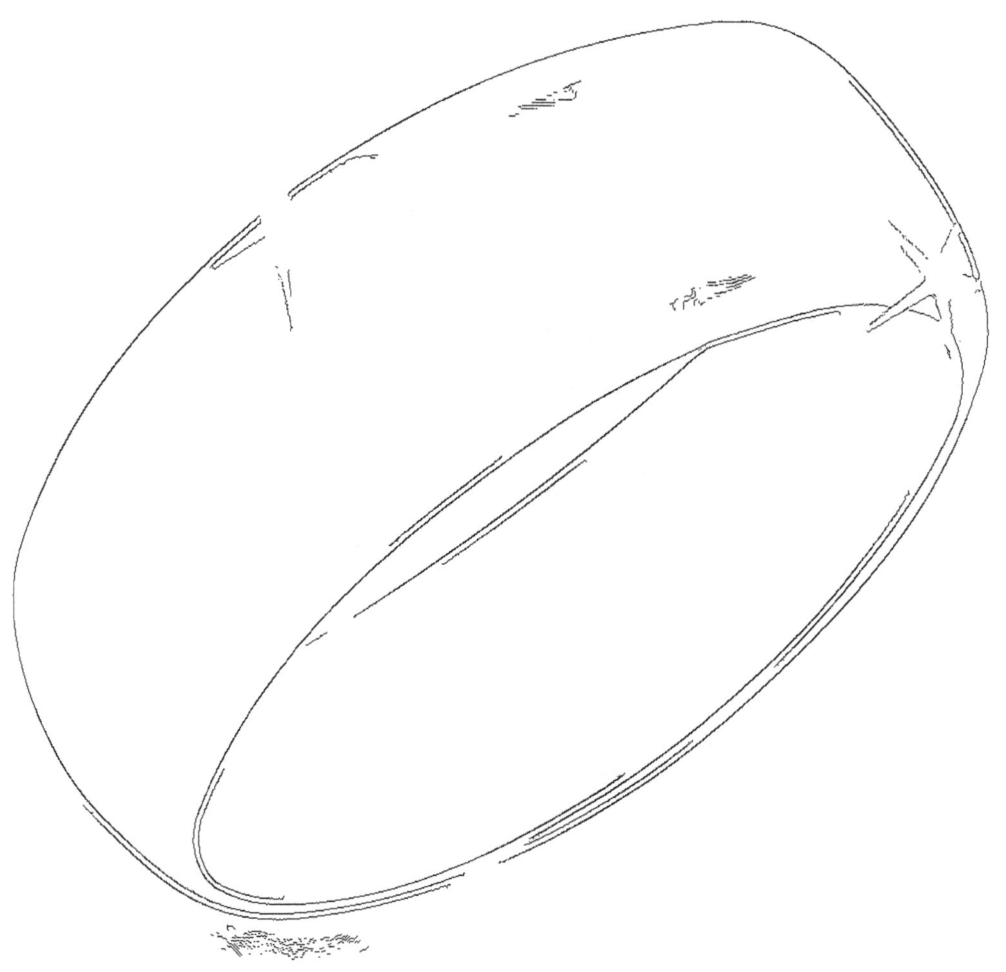

S

SOCK

T

TRACTOR

U

UNICORNE

V
VASE

W

WHALE

X

XYLOPHONE

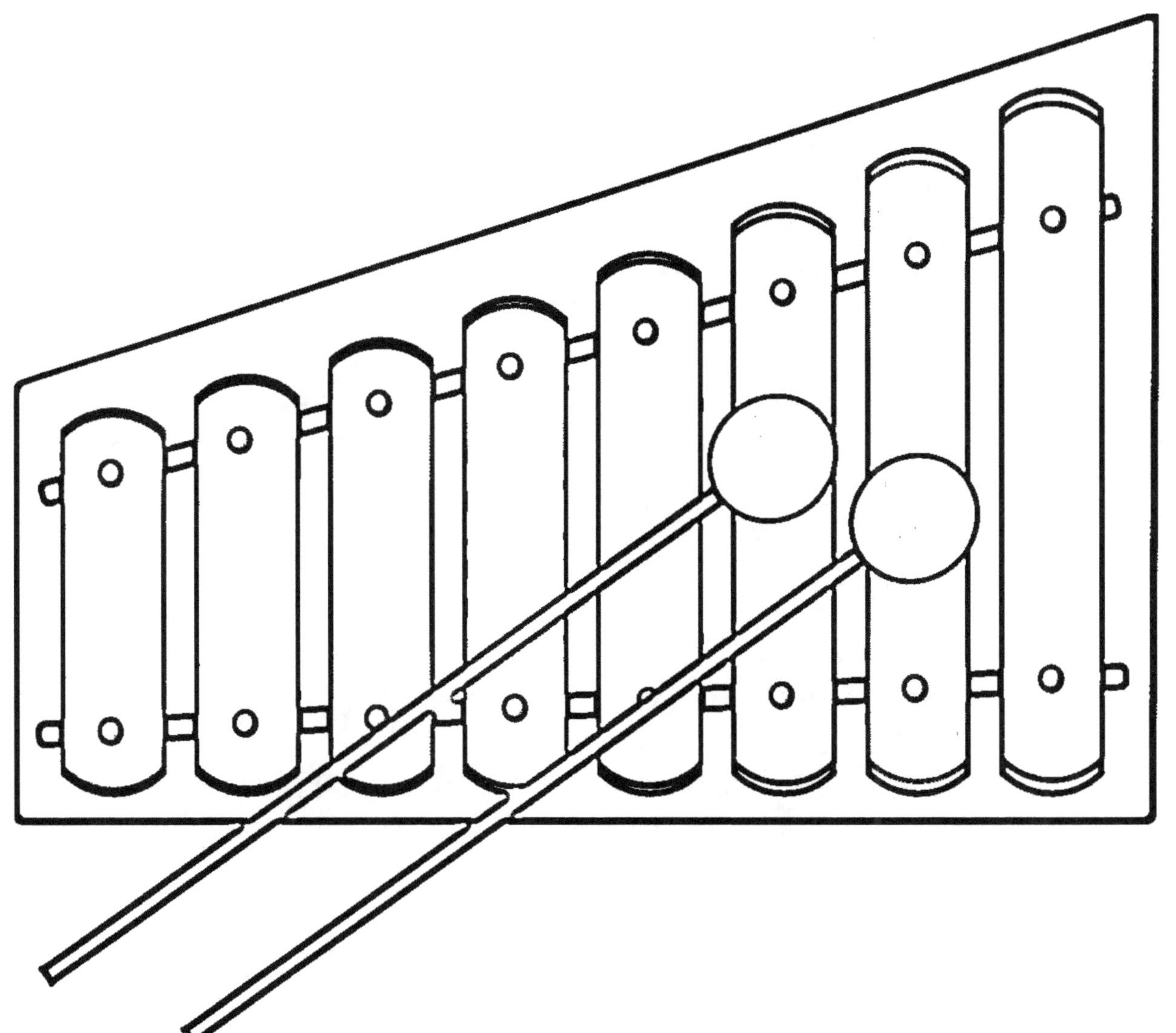

Y

YACHT

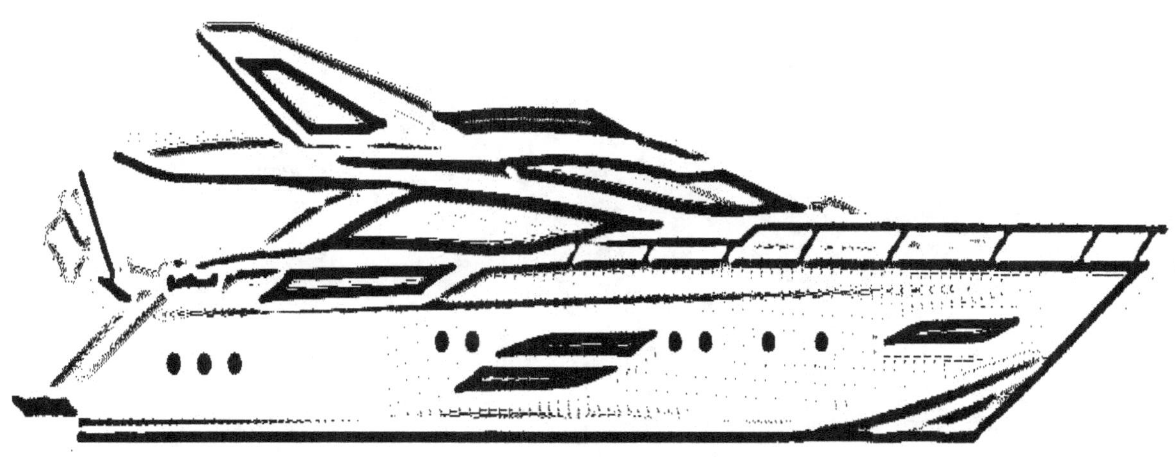

Z

ZEBRA